THE LIFE OF
ROSA PARKS

BY GILLIA M. OLSON

SEQUENCE

AMICUS | AMICUS INK

Sequence is published by Amicus and Amicus Ink
P.O. Box 227, Mankato, MN 56002
www.amicuspublishing.us

Library of Congress Cataloging-in-Publication Data
Names: Olson, Gillia M., author.
Title: The life of Rosa Parks / by Gillia M. Olson.
Description: Mankato, MN : Amicus, [2022] | Series: Sequence | Includes bibliographical references and index. | Audience: Ages 7-10 | Audience: Grades 2-3
Identifiers: LCCN 2019036304 (print) | LCCN 2019036305 (ebook) | ISBN 9781681519500 (library binding) | ISBN 9781681525976 (paperback) | ISBN 9781645490357 (pdf)
Subjects: LCSH: Parks, Rosa, 1913-2005–Juvenile literature. | African Americans–Alabama–Montgomery–Biography–Juvenile literature. | Civil rights workers–Alabama–Montgomery–Biography–Juvenile literature. | Montgomery (Ala.)–Biography–Juvenile literature. | African Americans–Civil rights–Alabama–Montgomery–Juvenile literature. | Segregation in transportation–Alabama–Montgomery–History--20th century–Juvenile literature. | Montgomery (Ala.)–Race relations–Juvenile literature.
Classification: LCC F334.M753 P38615 2022 (print) | LCC F334.M753 (ebook) | DDC 323.092 [B]–dc23
LC record available at https://lccn.loc.gov/2019036304
LC ebook record available at https://lccn.loc.gov/2019036305

Editor: Alissa Thielges
Designer: Ciara Beitlich
Photo Researcher: Marty Levick

Photo Credits: Shutterstock/Joseph Sohm cover; LOC/unknown cover, 8; Alamy/PictureLux/The Hollywood Archive 4; LOC/Wolcott, Marion Post 6–7; Getty/The Washington Post 8, 16; Newscom/Everett Collection 10–11; AP/Gene Herrick 12; Getty/Don Cravens 14–15; AP/uncredited 19; AP/Jim McKnight 20; AP/Associated Press 23; AP/Richard Sheinwald 24; LOC/Rosa Parks 26; Newscom/Jeff Kowalsky 26–27; AP/J. Scott Applewhite 28–29

TABLE OF CONTENTS

Rosa Parks was a life-long **activist** for civil rights.

LOADING...LOADING...LOADING...

Who was Rosa Parks?

In 1955, Rosa Parks chose not to give up her bus seat for a white man. As an African American, this was illegal. Rosa knew this. By staying seated, she stood up against racism. Her refusal inspired millions to work for equal rights. She is called the Mother of the **Civil Rights** Movement.

LOADING . . . LOADING . . . LOADING . . .

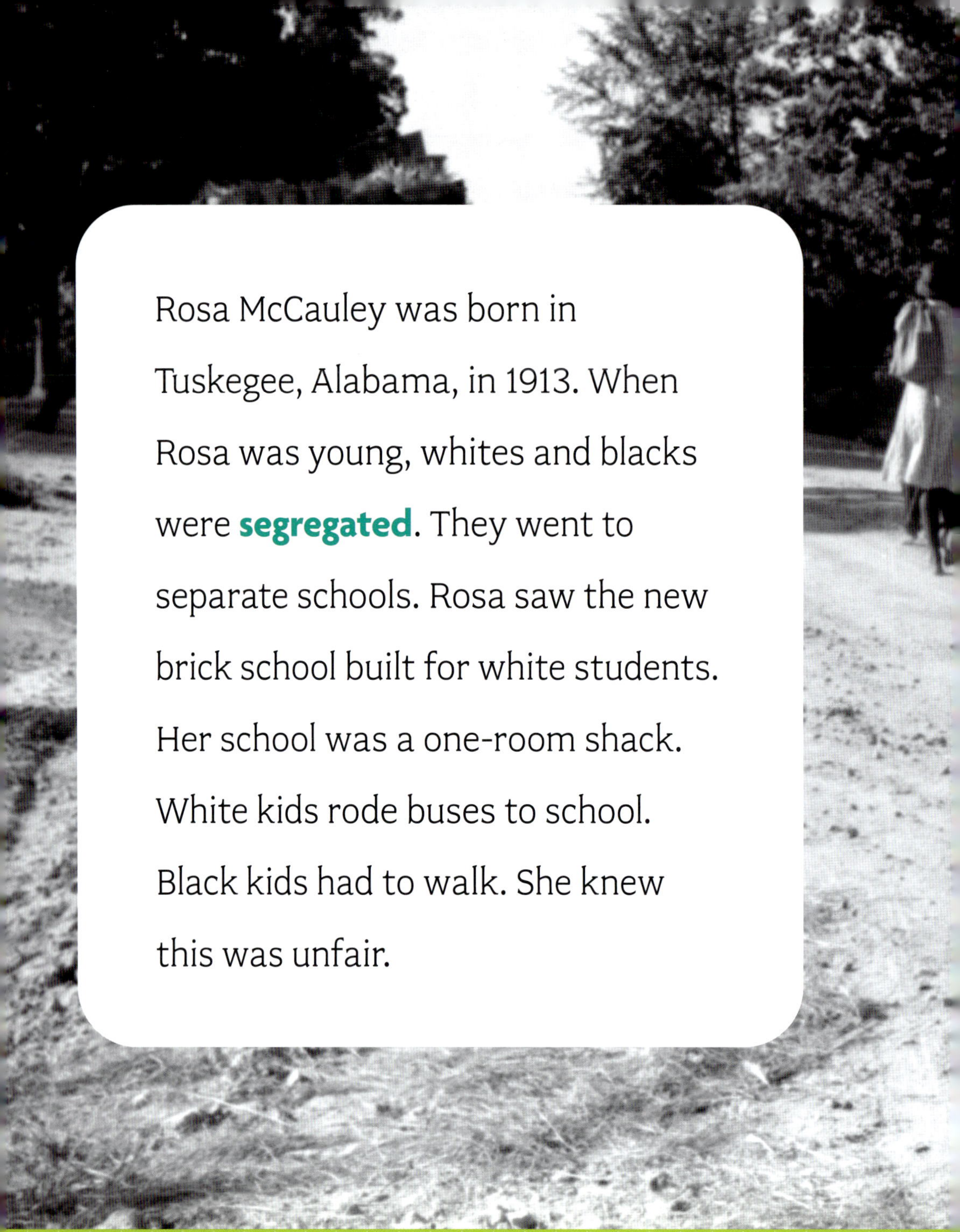

Rosa McCauley was born in Tuskegee, Alabama, in 1913. When Rosa was young, whites and blacks were **segregated**. They went to separate schools. Rosa saw the new brick school built for white students. Her school was a one-room shack. White kids rode buses to school. Black kids had to walk. She knew this was unfair.

Rosa McCauley is born.

FEB. 4, 1913

LOADING . . . LOADING . . .

Black children walk home from school on a dirt road in North Carolina.

Rosa was 19 when she married Raymond Parks. They were married for almost 45 years.

FEB. 4, 1913 — Rosa McCauley is born.

1932 — Rosa marries Raymond Parks.

DING . . . LOADING . . .

Early Activism

Rosa loved school. But as a teenager, she left school. She needed to care for her grandmother and mother.

Later, she joined the National Association for the Advancement of Colored People (NAACP). There she met Raymond Parks. He was a **volunteer** like her. They became friends. In 1932, they got married.

LOADING . . . LOADING . . . LOADING . . .

Rosa was elected **secretary** of the Montgomery NAACP in 1943. The group found fair legal help for people of color. Rosa helped black people sign up to vote. She learned how to organize for a cause. In 1949, she led the NAACP Youth Council. She taught young people how to be activists.

Young people in many states joined the NAACP. They protested segregation.

FEB. 4, 1913 — Rosa McCauley is born.

1932 — Rosa marries Raymond Parks.

1943 — Rosa is elected secretary of the Montgomery NAACP.

. . . LOADING . . .

LOADING... LOADING... LOADING...

Rosa gets her fingerprints taken after her second arrest in February 1956.

- FEB. 4, 1913: Rosa McCauley is born.
- 1932: Rosa marries Raymond Parks.
- 1943: Rosa is elected secretary of the Montgomery NAACP.
- DEC. 1, 1955: Rosa refuses to give up her bus seat to a white man.

The Bus Boycott

On December 1, 1955, Rosa was riding the bus home. Buses were segregated. There were separate white and black sections. On this day, the white section was full. When a white man came on board, there were no open seats. The bus driver told Rosa to give up her seat. It was the law. Rosa said no. The police were called. Rosa was arrested.

LOADING . . . LOADING . . . LOADING . . .

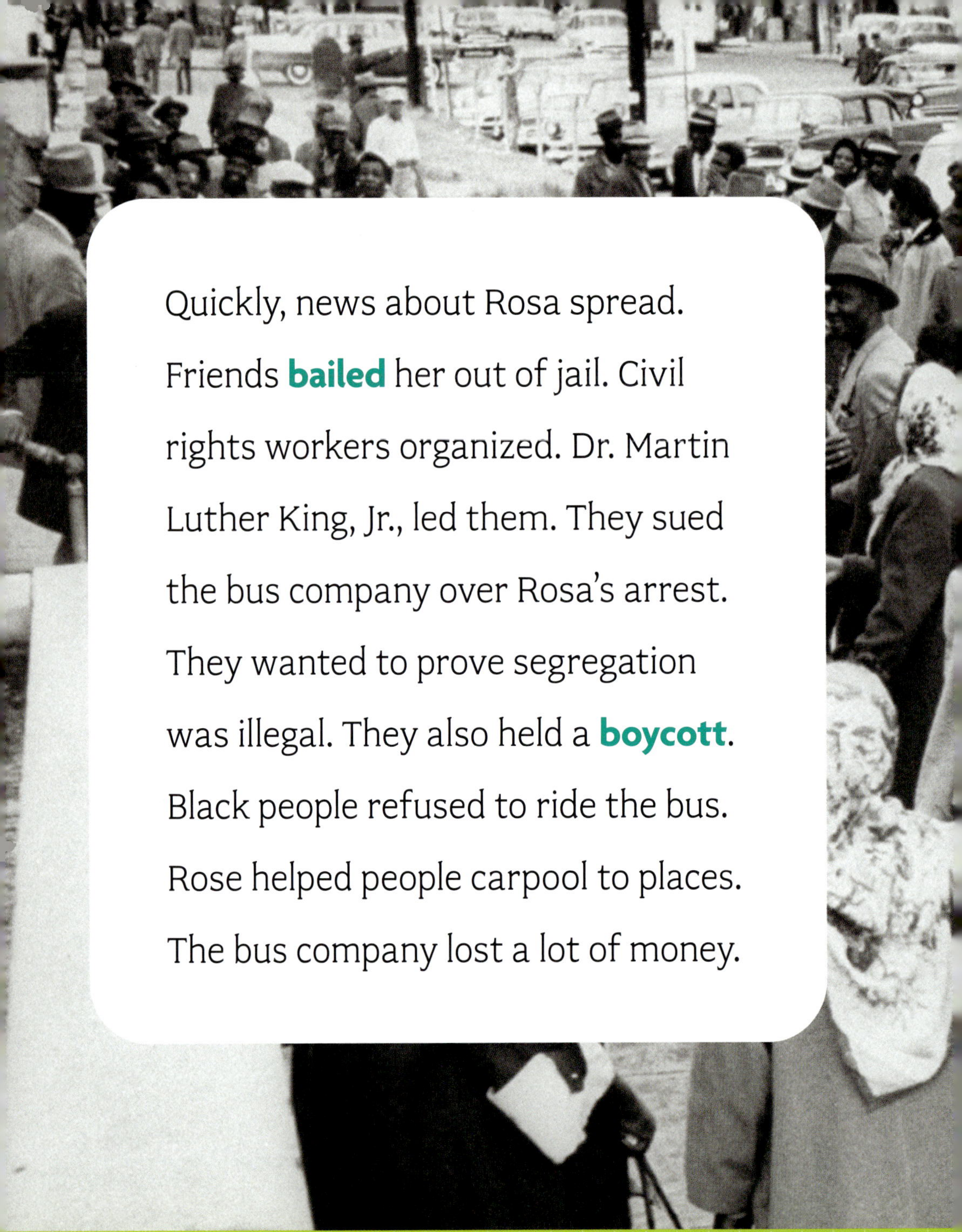

Quickly, news about Rosa spread. Friends **bailed** her out of jail. Civil rights workers organized. Dr. Martin Luther King, Jr., led them. They sued the bus company over Rosa's arrest. They wanted to prove segregation was illegal. They also held a **boycott**. Black people refused to ride the bus. Rose helped people carpool to places. The bus company lost a lot of money.

FEB. 4, 1913 — Rosa McCauley is born.

1932 — Rosa marries Raymond Parks.

1943 — Rosa is elected secretary of the Montgomery NAACP.

DEC. 1, 1955 — Rosa refuses to give up her bus seat to a white man.

DEC. 5, 1955 — The Montgomery bus boycott begins.

Black people gather in front of the Capitol Building during the bus boycott.

LOADING... LOADING... LOADING...

Rosa sits at the front of the bus at the end of the boycott.

- FEB. 4, 1913 — Rosa McCauley is born.
- 1932 — Rosa marries Raymond Parks.
- 1943 — Rosa is elected secretary of the Montgomery NAACP.
- DEC. 1, 1955 — Rosa refuses to give up her bus seat to a white man.
- DEC. 5, 1955 — The Montgomery bus boycott begins.
- 1956 — The Supreme Court ends segregation on public transportation.

At that time, boycotts were illegal. In 1956, Rosa and others were arrested. Rosa was fired from her **seamstress** job. The Parks got death threats. But they kept going. Finally, in 1956, the Supreme Court ruled on a case like Rosa's. Segregation on public transportation was ruled illegal. The boycott ended. It had lasted 381 days.

A Move North

In 1957, the Parks moved to Detroit, Michigan. Rosa's brother lived there. They continued their civil rights work. Rosa attended the March on Washington in 1963. She heard King's famous "I Have a Dream" speech. She also walked in the Selma-to-Montgomery March in 1965. It was for civil rights.

FEB. 4, 1913	Rosa McCauley is born.
1932	Rosa marries Raymond Parks.
1943	Rosa is elected secretary of the Montgomery NAACP.
DEC. 1, 1955	Rosa refuses to give up her bus seat to a white man.
DEC. 5, 1955	The Montgomery bus boycott begins.
1956	The Supreme Court ends segregation on public transportation.

Martin Luther King Jr. waves to the crowd before his speech in 1963.

The Parks move to Detroit, Michigan.

1957

. . L O A D I N G . . . L O A D I N G . . .

Rosa works as a secretary for U.S. Congressman John Conyers.

FEB. 4, 1913	Rosa McCauley is born.
1932	Rosa marries Raymond Parks.
1943	Rosa is elected secretary of the Montgomery NAACP.
DEC. 1, 1955	Rosa refuses to give up her bus seat to a white man.
DEC. 5, 1955	The Montgomery bus boycott begins.
1956	The Supreme Court ends segregation on public transportation.

Rosa got involved in politics. In 1965, she helped John Conyers get elected to Congress. He was one of the few African American congressmen. Rosa was hired as his secretary. She worked for him until 1988.

Rosa lost family members in the late 1970s. Raymond passed away in August 1977. In November, her brother passed away. Rosa's mother died in 1979.

The Parks move to Detroit, Michigan.

1957

1965

Rosa helps elect John Conyers to Congress.

LOADING . . . LOADING . . .

A Tireless Worker

Rosa was heartbroken over her losses. But her civil rights work gave her a purpose. She gave speeches. She continued to give people of color legal help. In 1979, the NAACP gave her the Spingarn Medal. It is the group's highest honor. In the 1980s, Rosa protested **apartheid** in South Africa. It was much like segregation in the United States.

Rosa holds a sign in a protest against South Africa's apartheid laws.

- FEB. 4, 1913 — Rosa McCauley is born.
- 1932 — Rosa marries Raymond Parks.
- 1943 — Rosa is elected secretary of the Montgomery NAACP.
- DEC. 1, 1955 — Rosa refuses to give up her bus seat to a white man.
- DEC. 5, 1955 — The Montgomery bus boycott begins.
- 1956 — The Supreme Court ends segregation on public transportation.

The Parks move to Detroit, Michigan.

Rosa helps elect John Conyers to Congress.

Awarded the NAACP Spingarn Medal, the group's highest honor.

1957

1965

1979

...LOADING...

Rosa McCauley is born.

FEB. 4, 1913

Rosa marries Raymond Parks.

1932

Rosa is elected secretary of the Montgomery NAACP.

1943

Rosa refuses to give up her bus seat to a white man.

DEC. 1, 1955

The Montgomery bus boycott begins.

DEC. 5, 1955

The Supreme Court ends segregation on public transportation.

1956

Rosa never had children. But she believed young people had power. They could make a change. In 1987, she started the Rosa and Raymond Parks Institute. It helps teenagers become leaders. It started the Pathways to Freedom bus tours. Students go around the country in buses. They visit important places of the civil rights movement.

A girl hugs Rosa at a ceremony to open a Pathways to Freedom school.

- 1957 — The Parks move to Detroit, Michigan.
- 1965 — Rosa helps elect John Conyers to Congress.
- 1979 — Awarded the NAACP Spingarn Medal, the group's highest honor.
- 1987 — Rosa founds the Rosa and Raymond Parks Institute.

OADING . . .

In 1995, Rosa wrote a book called *Quiet Strength*, shown in the inset photo. It talks about her life and her work for equal rights.

By the 1990s, Rosa had worked for civil rights for decades. She was awarded the Presidential Medal of Freedom in 1996 for her tireless work. In 1999, she also received the Congressional Medal of Honor.

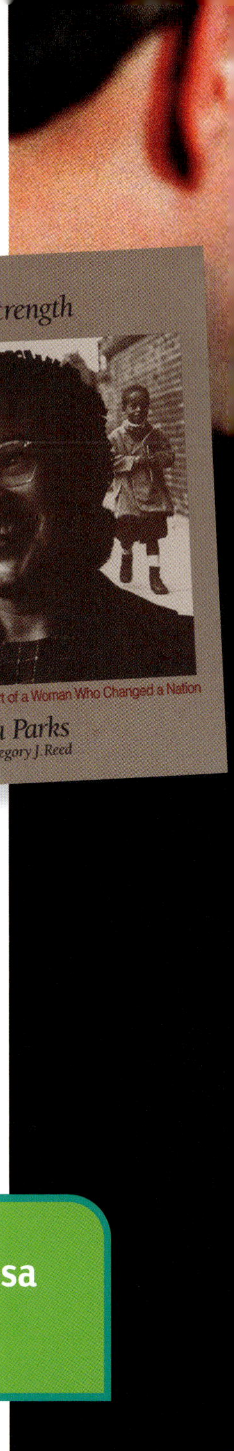

Vice President Al Gore hands Rosa the Medal of Honor.

- FEB. 4, 1913 — Rosa McCauley is born.
- 1932 — Rosa marries Raymond Parks.
- 1943 — Rosa is elected secretary of the Montgomery NAACP.
- DEC. 1, 1955 — Rosa refuses to give up her bus seat to a white man.
- DEC. 5, 1955 — The Montgomery bus boycott begins.
- 1956 — The Supreme Court ends segregation on public transportation.

The Parks move to Detroit, Michigan.

1957

Awarded the NAACP Spingarn Medal, the group's highest honor.

1965

Rosa helps elect John Conyers to Congress.

1979

1987

Rosa founds the Rosa and Raymond Parks Institute.

1995

Rosa publishes her memoir, *Quiet Strength*.

NG . . .

FEB. 4, 1913	1932	1943	DEC. 1, 1955	DEC. 5, 1955	1956
Rosa McCauley is born.	Rosa marries Raymond Parks.	Rosa is elected secretary of the Montgomery NAACP.	Rosa refuses to give up her bus seat to a white man.	The Montgomery bus boycott begins.	The Supreme Court ends segregation on public transportation.

Rosa passed away in 2005 at age 92. Her body laid in honor at the Capitol in Washington, D.C. She was the first woman honored this way. A statue of her was placed in Statuary Hall. People remember her as a civil rights leader. For 70 years, this quiet, strong woman worked for equal rights. She reminds us to never stop creating a better world for all people.

Rosa Parks' bronze statue shows how she looked on the day of her first arrest.

- **1957** The Parks move to Detroit, Michigan.
- **1965** Rosa helps elect John Conyers to Congress.
- **1979** Awarded the NAACP Spingarn Medal, the group's highest honor.
- **1987** Rosa founds the Rosa and Raymond Parks Institute.
- **1995** Rosa publishes her memoir, *Quiet Strength*.
- **2005** Rosa dies and lies in honor at the U.S. Capitol.

Glossary

activist Someone who works to bring about a political or social change.

apartheid A policy of racial separation enforced by South Africa's government from 1948 until the early 1990s.

bail To deposit money to free someone from jail, as a promise that the person will later appear in court.

boycott To refuse to buy from a company or brand to force them to meet demands.

civil rights The right of citizens to have equality, no matter their race, religion, or gender.

seamstress A woman who sews, especially as a job.

secretary A person who is in charge of keeping records and making appointments.

segregate To keep people separate by race, for example separating people by race into different schools.

volunteer Someone who works without pay.

Read More

Patrick, Denise Lewis. *A Girl Named Rosa: The True Story of Rosa Parks.* New York: Scholastic, 2018.

Ruiz, Rachel. *When Rosa Parks Went Fishing.* North Mankato, Minn.: Capstone, 2018.

Stoltman, Joan. *Rosa Parks.* New York: Gareth Stevens Publishing, 2018.

Websites

An Interview with Rosa Parks
https://www.achievement.org/achiever/rosa-parks/#interview

Nat Geo Kids | The Life of Rosa Parks
https://www.natgeokids.com/uk/discover/history/general-history/rosa-parks/

PBS Learning Media: Rosa Parks
https://www.pbslearningmedia.org/resource/americon-vid-rosa-parks/video/

Every effort has been made to ensure that these websites are appropriate for children. However, because of the nature of the Internet, it is impossible to guarantee that these sites will remain active indefinitely or that their contents will not be altered.

Index

About the Author

Gillia M. Olson is a former farm girl turned writer. She's written and edited children's books for more than 20 years. She hopes stories of great women will inspire her daughter someday, just as they have inspired her. She lives in southern Minnesota.